The Bus Rid

"Tom,"
said Grandpa.
"Let's play *I Spy*.
I spy something
that starts with **w**."

2

3

"Is it waterfall?"
said Tom.
"Yes," said Grandpa.

4

"I spy something that starts with **m**," said Tom.

"Is it mountain?"
said Grandpa.
"Yes," said Tom.

8

"I spy something that starts with I," said Grandpa.

11

"Is it lightning?"
said Tom.
"Yes," said Grandpa.

13

14

"I spy something
that starts with **b**, **bl**, and **cl**,"
said Tom.
"What?" said Grandpa.

"Big, black clouds,"
said Tom.
Grandpa laughed.

17

"I spy something
that starts with **r**,"
said Grandpa.

19

"Is it rainbow?"
said Tom.
"Yes," said Grandpa.

"And I spy something that starts with **gr**," said Grandpa.

23

"Grandma!" said Tom.